PHILOMATH
Sweetener
SUNRISES

LAUREN DANAE TRUMAN

MILTON & HUGO L.L.C.
4407 Park Ave., Suite 5
Union City, NJ 07087, USA

Website: *www. miltonandhugo.com*
Hotline: *1- 888-778-0033*
Email: *info@miltonandhugo.com*

Ordering Information:
Quantity sales. Special discounts are granted to corporations, associations, and other organizations. For more information on these discounts, please reach out to the publisher using the contact information provided above.

Library of Congress Control Number: IN-PROCESS
ISBN-13:   979-8-89285-092-6   [Paperback Edition]
                   979-8-89285-093-3   [Hardback Edition]
                   979-8-89285-094-0   [Digital Edition]

Rev. date: 04/16/2024

This book is for the romantics searching for
the right words to say. For those who pay
attention to detail. For those who feel immensely
in depth with the world and poetry.
Hope you all enjoy.

Contents

To Be Loved

To be loved at the highest count.
It's breathing in sunshine that I can only feel.
It's the pink skies hidden in laughter.
It's warm rays in my bones.
Two past lives could never come between us.
It's the feeling of safety and scared in the same length.
It's speaking in silence and never losing contentment.
It's crisp mornings that bring warmth to the love.
It's delicacy bleeding between two souls.
To be loved at the highest count.

Rain

You are rain to me.
You soothe me in every endearing way possible.
The touch of you makes me shiver,
raising the hairs on my body.
Everlasting, yet thrilling in the same way.
The sound of you fills me with an
infinite happiness to be alone.
To love you with no exchanges nor expectations.
I would never want to live a day where I can't hear you.
I dread the day you stop touching me.
Existing.
I smell you in every way possible.
Let me drown in you.
Drench me in the comfort and love it brings.
You are rain to me.

Dying Flowers

To feel the pain of loving you, is to
die a million deaths alone.
And yet, the stars will continue to shine for you.
The highest sound of love is written in your name.
Let my ashes grow from the rain of your spirit.
In afterlife, lay my body to rest and may
I ever be always grown by you.
Wilted tulips surround the grave.
Tell me that you love me more than hate.
Don't wait till I die to finally yearn for me.
I am already mourning the world without you.

Hopeful

To be in love is a risk, it's never stagnant.

Lovers May Dream

In my sleep, you come back to me.
Dreaming in a substance where my
hope never turned false.
In my sleep, you carry my worries
and heal my open wounds.
Let me be numb, high off a painless amnesia.
Praying I don't awake and remember
the agony without you.
Emerging from this sleepy world, I am drenched in sadness,
-restless and gasping for air-
In my dreams, there are pink skies and you love me.
Heaven is a place on Earth with you.
I can't help to say it feels like death.
Gray skies came back, and my rose-
colored glasses have broke.
Please do not let me wake,
For I long to be on the realm with you.

If my dreams go black and I'm cursed to not remember,
I pray I visit your dreams this lonely night.
Dear God, as I lay my head down to rest, I pray I visit
the dreams of the beautiful soul I have seen to love.
I pray in this mysterious land, you let my voice be heard.
To tell him he is, and will, become
everything I hoped he'd be.
To mend his heart and to feed his soul with
only the most graciousness of gold love.

I pray in this dream; my hands show patience to
touch the light surrounding his mind and never
let his blood shed the depth of darkness.
I pray to you on this lonely night to let
me be with him in his dreams.
Let me tell him all the words I have left in my language.
With every ounce my beating heart
spills, let it spill for him.
Let my hourglass of counting sand drain, if it means him.
In this dream, all his fears and agony vanish as they are.
Let his life be shared with me for just a moment.
Let me freeze your time, Lord.
Dear God, whether my love sleeps or shall
be wake, let me celebrate his existence.
I pray to you tonight God as I lay my head
down, in no matter what world, no matter what
realm, you will let him know he is loved.
If he shall wake and forget about me,
let me live on in his dreams.
I pray to you, you shall let him sleep, and come back to me.

Wine

Is he making your glass half empty?
Or are you his glass half full?
Why is it death?
Death of a broken heart.
Death of a lost soul.
Death of the consequences to stop feeling love.
Death of the empty wine bottle.
Every taste of grape on my lips, I remember,
You were so enamored with me.

Headaches

Headaches seem to cave-in when you enter my mind.
Please go away.
Please go back to my frozen time of love.
Where nothing mattered and you didn't hurt me.
Or maybe go back to when you didn't exist,
but I can't say that.
Because falling in love with you was breathtaking.
It was being alive.
And I'm trying so hard to live.

Wallowed Love Notes

If I ever loved you less, then I might
be able to talk about it more.
Not a day goes by when I haven't thought of
you, and now that I love you, I'm in agony.
I'm haunted every moment on this Earth by pieces of you.
Unconditional from one side, as they say.
Breaking my chest,
Breathless, thinking of how I lost you.
We are under the same moon, and yet,
It's two hearts living in two separate worlds.
It is no sacrifice when it comes to you.

I'm Worth the Risk

There's a knife in my throat when I want
to say the words I miss you.
Would you rather be comfortable or happy?

Sunlight

I can still see it all in my head.
And I can still feel it all on my skin.
I smell it through the breeze, and I hear it in the birds.
His hello was a beginning to all my endings.
And my laugh is what he had been missing.
I always believed love was black and gray, before,
I had never been happier to be wrong.
With him, love was the golden sun.

Cold Oregon Mornings

The smell of him was scented miles away.
It's engraved in my lungs and imprinted on my skin.
I am taunted by his voice; it has been my favorite sound.
My musical for the rest of eternity.
Laughter only I can hear,
Stuck in a love, expect I am the only one there.

Shedding You

They say it takes about a month to have
your top layer of your skin shed behind and
get renewed by your bottom layer.
I dread shredding you away as I touch something.
My lips will no longer feel yours.
My fingers will never have your skin imprinted on them.
Your touch will forever be erased from my neck and back.
Isn't that the saddest thing you've ever heard?

Dreamer

I love you in all my dreams.

Never Ending

I cried for everything I couldn't say, and
for things I didn't even know I felt.
All roads will forever and only lead to you:
Even the ones I drastically try to follow, just to forget you.

Birmingham

I painted you a blue sky, but you turned it into rain.
Embedded into my lungs, you are my first love.
Carved onto my skin with every raise screams your name.
Imprinted on every single bone, my blood rushes for you.
My heart shall beat to the meaning of you.
It's a million deaths to lose you.
It's burn to a flickering flame to grow with you.
Im begging you, take my hand and shield
me from the cold breezes of May.
I bathe in cliffside pools with the golden faith of loving you.
If words could just hold you, tell me you'd feel me.
If that is all I'll ever get.

Morning Cuddles

What is more than love?
Cinnamon honey tea, almost as sweet as him.
Coconut rum mojito makes me think of him.
Only time to cry is to laugh with him.
My dreamer love bug wrapped into my heart tight.
Pour me sunlight and kiss me a million goodnights.

My Love for the Birds

And do you think they miss us?
When we are no longer on the bench.
When we no longer exist in their time.
Just as my heart pines for their sound of chirps.
Do they miss us like I miss them?
Do they miss us like I miss you?
Do they still sing when we're not
around to hear the melody.
I dream of a version of you that I might
not have had, but I did not lose.
'I miss you' feels like death in my throat.
It's the anchor of my days that I can't seem to say.
I'm petrified of the weather because I hear you in the rain.
I see you in the sun, and I feel you in my agony of pain.
No measure of time is long enough to love you.
And no measure of uncertainty could
ever be able to stop me.

Happy Birthday

I couldn't love you more than I do right
now, and yet tomorrow I shall.
I once said to be alive and loved is to feel joy.
You are the definition of joy.
You are inside of me; with every breath I take.
You are my warmth in the cold mornings.
You are everything Heaven on Earth is.
I'll forever recognize you in darkness.
If I were to be deaf and you mute,
I would recognize your joy.
Thirty-six years of you in life.
How wonderfully blessed to be alive with you.
To have met in a past life or the next,
I will always, honestly, truly, completely
be in love with you.
It will always be you.
Let's start with forever.
Happiest of birthdays to my love bug.

Tangled Threads

You make me never want to love again.
Our souls didn't meet on accident.
It's as if you were wounded, or yet maybe I.
You are the best thing that has ever been mine.
Our souls are lovers that forever will lie.
Besides, intertwined, melted, it will never die.
Cobble stones around your heart, wet by the
rain, only thing to see has been gray.
Sunshine seeps through your words, and
it's the only language I understand.
Colors of love that only you and I can see.

Breathtaking

To freely live.
To love you, is to stand for all the things I was made for.
I vow to you; I will make up all the
years we never had together.
A little bit of you, lives in everything I love.
I am who I love, and I continue to grow
exceptionally in love with you.
I love you in every way there is to bleed.
To heal all wounds, would never compare
to the epiphany it was to meet you.
I'd give up forever to touch you,
To hold you in life and smell your
everlasting scent on Earth.
To cherish your voice, as if I shall be blind,
I will always come back to you.
To love you, is to meet you in the next life.
Where my soul will never forget you.
To love you, is freeing.

Love After Death

Birds of love,
Endless laughter.
If I froze time, will you forever be mine?
Our souls are lovers.
We shall never die.
The folk songs of my heart will forever weep your name.
You and I.
My words will forever be the permanent
ink that will last beyond my grave.

Enough

If love was enough.
If love was enough, you would have chosen me.
If love was enough, you would never look away.
If love was enough.

Pottery and Clay

Pages turn and they stick together.
It's so hard not to love you during this weather.
I am hopeless, breathless, burning slow.
Please grab me, tell me you'll never let me go.
I don't want to have to do anything without you.
My tears ricochet in the forever moonlight sadness of you.
If a million shall ever love you, I will be one.
If only one loves you, it has only been me.
Tell me you've longed and would never leave.
If you were born earlier and I later, we
would have walked this Earth alone.
Whatever our souls are made out of, I'd
like to think we are the same.

Imagine

A life where I'm not a crumpled-up
letter missing the eyes of you.
A life where I'm not paralyzed while
time moves on from you.
A life where I'm never a secret, yet I am
the same oath I pledge to you.
A life where we won't ever get lost in the communication.
A life where I'm far from hell every-
time you double cross my mind.
A life where I shall never feel you forget
me, like I used to feel you breathe.
A life where it is me.

Forgetting Me

It's death by a thousand cuts, hearing your name.
Maybe it will be better if you say you didn't love me at all.
Maybe it would be better if you just forgot my name.
Will my tears ever stop?
I lay down and dream of a realm where you loved me.
One where you never forget me.
How could I ever not touch you again?

Rainy Graves

I see you in the storms, those rainy Sunday evenings.
I feel it on my pale skin as I miss your touch.
I smell you miles away.
I am afraid I'll never forget your scent.
Loving you is haunting me.
Or is it taunting?
I will forever be mourning you alone.
Visiting our rainy graves.

My Snakeskin

Why did you shed my skin and take my innocence.
I felt like a virgin brand new with you.
I never thought you would make me feel used.
Waste me and throw it away.
I was expendable to your happiness
and it makes me hate myself.
Even more than what I already hated.

Day Dreaming

I am so agitated by my sadness.
I can't seem to sit alone with the thoughts of you.

After You

Where does the love go?
Does it fade into existence or does it melt onto your skin.
Does it disappear as the ash does from the flame?
Does it take a piece of me when it leaves?
What happens to the joy in my laugh?
Does it slowly fade, as you faded from me?
Does it reside in your lungs, rest in your bones?
Will I ever get it back?
Will I ever get you back?

Time Won't Heal

Don't ever tell me how long it should take me to heal.
How long is should take to get over you.
It was real to me.
Every ounce of it.

Frozen

I am taunted by your voice.
It used to be my favorite sound.
Frozen by your laughter.
Shivering from your presence.
Listening to your demons.
Wrapped in the melody of your sighs.
Now when I come across your sound, I am frozen.
Stuck in a place of love.
Except I am the only one here.

Happy Fourth

It's the Fourth of July and I am alone.
Are you out there?
Thinking of me under the same dusky sky.
Withering feathers that breeze by.
Drifting wind will only come between you and me.
Fireworks you and I can hear, but never see.

Thrift Store

Anything will feel better, compared to him not loving me.
Was I put on Earth to give my love freely?
No exchanges nor transactions.
Is that how priceless my love was for him?
A good-will thrift shop, all I ever was.
Why wasn't my love ever valuable?
Was I just not the right color of price
tag needed at the time.
It's okay, put me back on the rack.

Self Love

Avoidance is the only way you knew how to love me.
But I loved you, no avoidance necessary.
That was the only way I desperately
knew how to love myself.

Listening Half Way

You told me a thousand ways that you loved me.
Yet, you told me a million ways that you didn't want me.
Why can I only remember the first portion?
Why haven't I let you go?

Losing the Sunrise

Pink and orange skies will forever pour your name.
You are embedded into my skin.
Can you feel it when I am touching you?
When my hair stands it's saluting you.
The pigment in my cheeks only blush to you.
The butterflies will only ever fly for you.
The sunrise shall shine if our love is true.
The moon dies as my wined dressed dries.
Maybe the blue can turn into something beautiful too.

Lonely Sunsets

I absolutely dread the sun coming down.
Why do I have to feel the pain that follows.
The tears that lingered.
Why can't the sky remain in your name?
Pink and full of love and laughter.
Why did your love end for me as the day did.
Do you think the sun tells the moon
"Good night and I love you?"
Does it respond with "I love you too."

Seal Rock After Me

You try to bathe in this shore and
pretend we didn't fall apart.
Pretending we didn't break each other's hearts.
Since you admitted it, I can see it.
Looking over at you, looking at me.
How does it feel that my love slipped beyond your reach?
Evergreen, do you mourn for me?
Busy streets and blowing breeze.
There's an ache in you, when you're wondering of me.
Beyond the cries and pleading.
It hurts to laugh without me.
Just as it could have been love, I will
be your forever memory.
The spelling of pain, seeing the words of my name.
And you're still sitting in the garden I haunt.
If it's all in my head, please tell me I'm wrong.
Do you remember that Wednesday night?
It was the first time you ever saw me.
Planning of the ocean Seal Rock and rings.

And now it's devastating to lose me for you.
Bowing to my words as the sun does to the moon.
Feeling my love with closed eyes as the
ocean can feel you breathe.
Riptides through your chest to the path of my heart.
Yearning and solitude clenching your mind.
You dropped my hand and sand collected on your legs.
Left in your own fantasy, after me.
And I'm still here, where you left me.

Hopeless

I am so dramatically heartbroken. It hurts my soul.

Drunk Thoughts

I wish I was who you drunk texted at midnight.
I wonder if I cross your mind half as much as you do mine.

Self Inflicted

There's no weight to the love you are giving me.
If I say I miss you, I know that you won't.
And I miss you in the morning when I see the sun.
I will never get away from you.
And maybe I don't want to.

Please

It's the broken promises I needed so badly to be true.

Green Eyes

Green eyes.
Green eyes haunt me forever now.
I will always look for you.
The green eyes that loved me so.
The green eyes that saw right through me.
The green eyes that made me warm.
That fed me love.
My green eyes forever you will be to me.

Amore

I love you to the point of ruin.
Until my lungs are filled with ash.
My barron land only surrounded with hopeless love.
Take me where all the poets died.
Gushing cold along the lakes of tears.
What should have passed is buried under my skin.
My sleepless nights and your faithless
love are what I believed in.
Yet, I only want your shade of blue.
Say what I can't speak about.
Trying to answer the question of how I could
ever look away now that I have seen you.

Blow Out Your Candles

May all your wishes come true, even
the ones that don't include me.

Before Me

For my hands to remember your skin.
For my lips to remember your lips.
For my head to remember not to hurt anymore.
For me to remember loving you.
And for you to remember life before me.

No Measure Of Time

No measure of time will ever be long enough with you.
Kiss me in its entirety and feed my naked soul.
Enlighten me with your breath of reliefs,
And forever burn the candle between.
Let it desperately hurt to ever live a life without me.
If I shall be blind, I'd live beautifully by your sound.
I am forever melted in your love completely.

Lost in Translation

My love for you is Heaven, before you even get there.
Melt into me like snow so you can forever hold me.
Dissolve with me so you can forever kiss me.
Render with me so you can forever love me.
I can love you with a broken heart.
I vow to never be half in love.
Bury me next to you,
I am utterly in love.
I can learn every language and still wouldn't
be able to tell you how much I love you.
I can read every book on poetry and never come
close to the sadness of not having you.